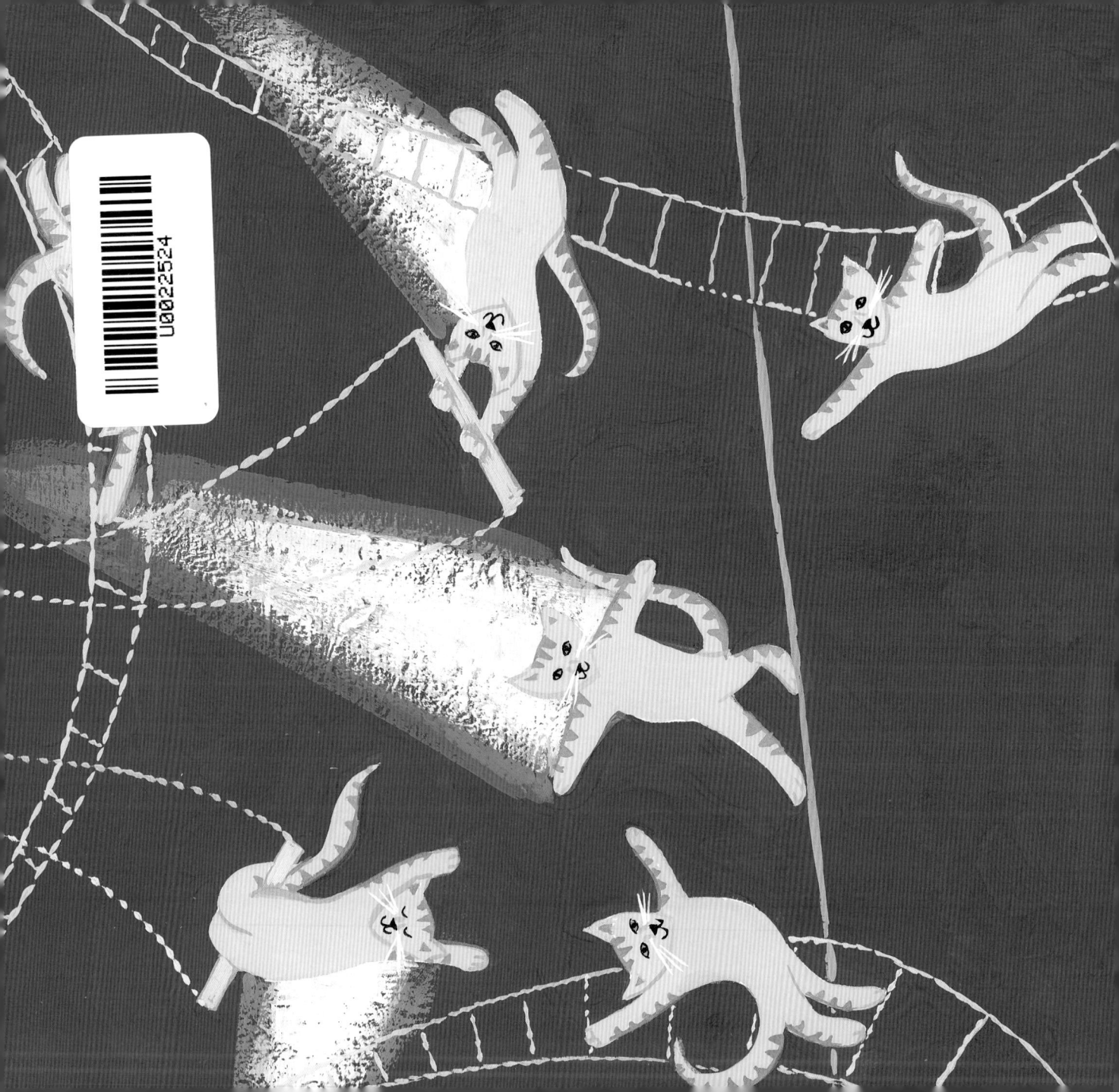

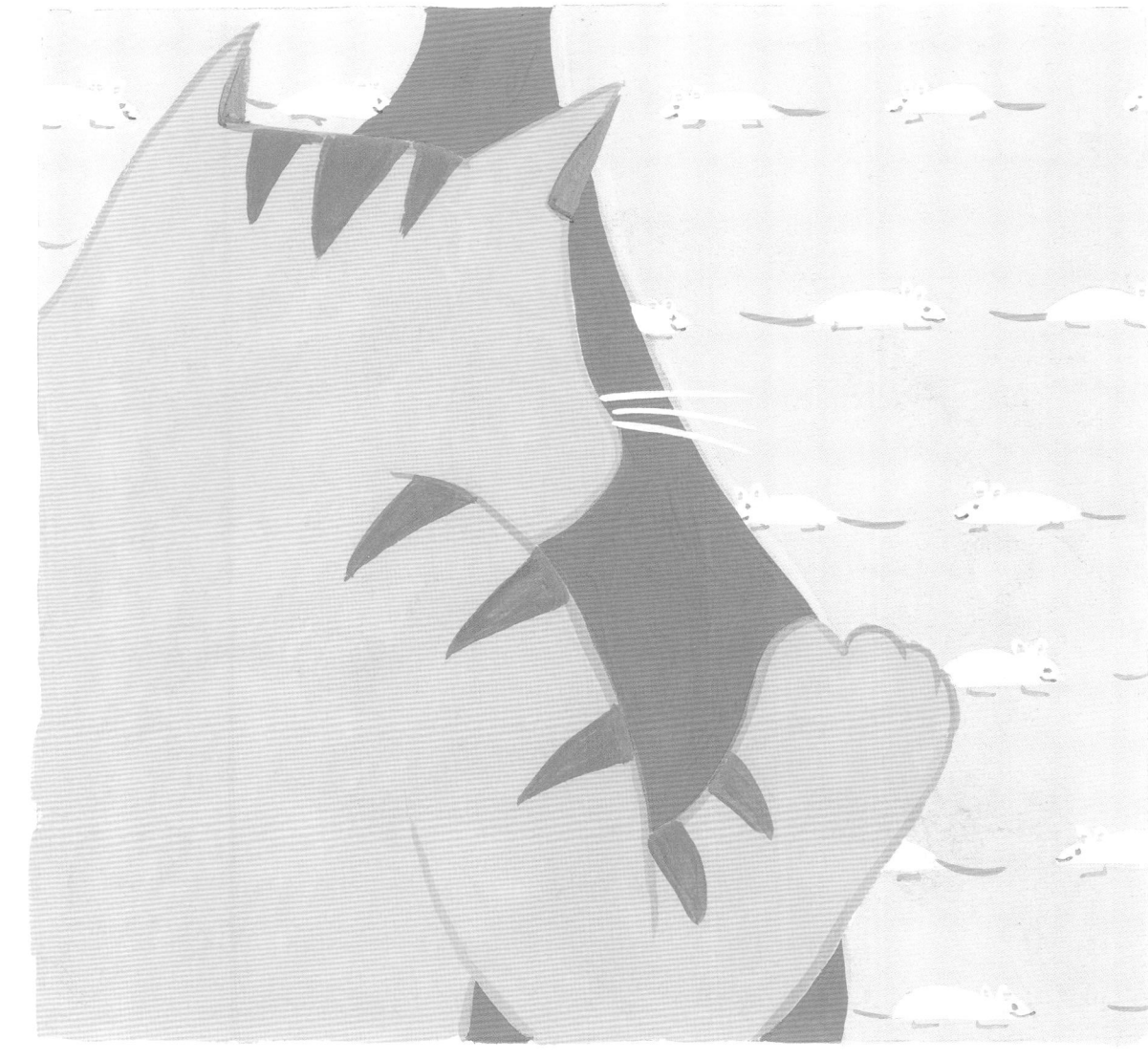

One morning Zippy hears music. He looks out of the window.

People and animals are dancing in the street. They are
*dressed up for a *celebration.

He follows them to a tent.

Zippy goes inside.

This cat has green eyes, just like Zippy.

This cat has *whiskers just like Zippy. But, Zippy thinks, this cat is *as tall as a house!

A woman is holding a *hoop and the big cat jumps through it.

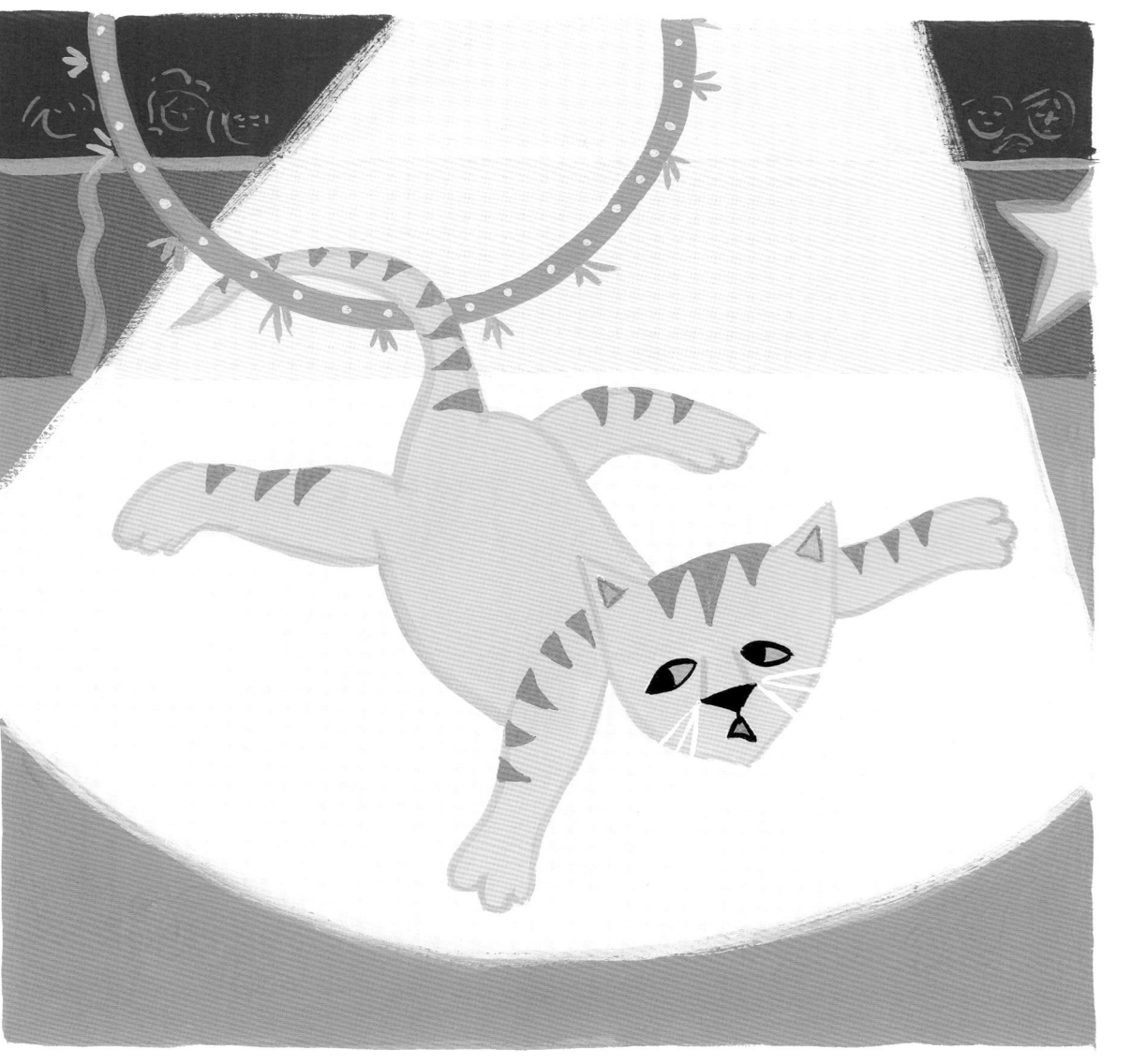

Zippy is so excited that he tries to follow the big cat through the hoop. He falls down. He *lands on his tummy.

The big cat shakes her head. She jumps through the hoop.
She makes it look easy to do.

"MEOW," cries Zippy. He tries again.

This time when he follows the big cat he seems to fly.

And there, on the *front page, is a picture of Zippy and the
very big cat.

生字表

n.= 名詞，v.= 動詞

賽西莉逛馬戲團

⭐ *p.10*
他在看帳篷四周，簡直不敢相信他的眼睛！
在帳篷的中央打了一道光束。
他的眼光聚燈下，有一一隻超級大貓。

⭐ *p.11*
這隻貓身上的斑紋，跟賽皮的好像。

⭐ *p.12*
牠的綠色眼睛，跟賽皮的也很像。

⭐ *p.13*
牠還有跟賽皮一樣的鬍鬚。
這隻貓就像房子一樣高！

⭐ *p.14*
有一個女人手上拿著一個圈圈，這隻大貓穿越圈圈跳了過去。

⭐ *p.15*
賽皮非常興奮，他試著要跟隨著大貓穿越圈圈。
可是他跌倒了，肚子著著地。

⭐ *p.16*
大貓搖了搖頭。她又一穿越圈圈圈跳了過去，一副
很輕鬆的樣子。

p.17

賽皮大叫：「喵！」然後，他再試一次。這一次，他跟著大貓穿越圈圈的時候，好像飛了起來！

p.18

他降落在大貓的背上，鞠了一個躬。

p.19

大家都好喜歡賽皮的表演！他們鼓掌大喊：「好聰明的貓！」

p.20

當賽皮回到家時，他簡直累壞了，直接倒頭大睡，也沒有打電話給柔依。

p.21

但是隔天早上，太陽一升起來，柔依馬上打電話給賽皮。她告訴賽皮：「今天的報紙上，有你的照片呢！」

p.22

的確，就在頭版上，有一張賽皮與超級大貓的照片。

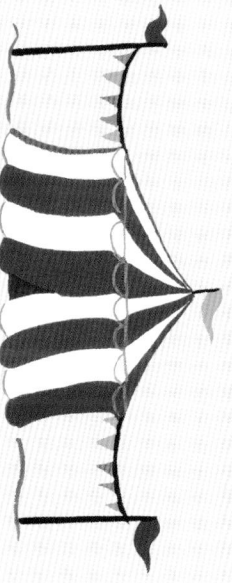

認識馬戲團

小朋友，你曾經看過馬戲團的表演嗎？如果有，什麼樣的表演讓你印象最深刻呢？請跟著一起做下面的練習，讓我們來認識馬戲團吧！

Part. 1

請聽 CD 的 Track 4，唸出這些有關馬戲團的英文單字：

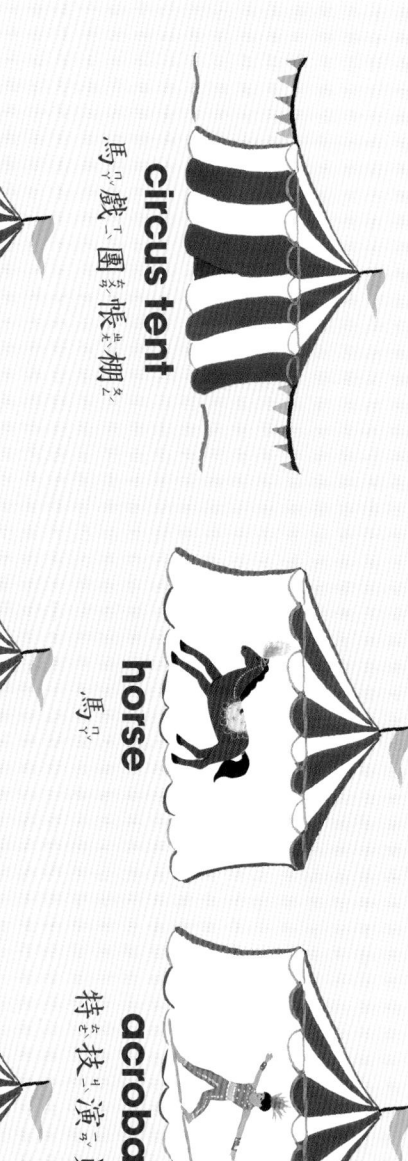

circus tent
馬戲團帳棚

horse
馬

tiger
老虎

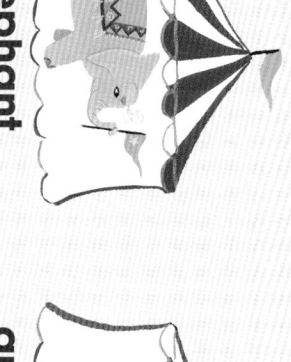

elephant
大象

acrobat
特技演員

animal trainer
馴獸師

27

Part. 2 下面這篇文章，是索依在報紙上看到關於馬戲團歷險的新聞報導。請根據第 27 頁的英文單字和下面的提示圖，圈出正確的單字。（正確的答案在第 29 頁喔！）

Cat Times

Zippy the cat performed in a circus yesterday. Yesterday morning Zippy heard music. He saw **(animal trainers/ acrobats)** and  **(an elephant/a horse)** in the street. He was so interested that he followed the parade. In the center of a tent Zippy found a VERY big cat—it's a **(horse/ tiger)**! She jumped through a hoop and Zippy jumped through the hoop too! Zippy landed on the big cat's back and took a bow. The people were happy and said, "What a clever cat?"

活⟨ㄏㄨㄛˊ⟩動⟨ㄉㄨㄥˋ⟩解⟨ㄐㄧㄝˇ⟩答⟨ㄉㄚˊ⟩：
acrobats, an elephant, tiger

Zippy likes to jump. He jumps onto the chair. He jumps from the chair to the table. He jumps from the table to the couch. Sometimes he even jumps to the top of the refrigerator.

I love the circus. When I see Zippy jump I think he looks like a "Circus Cat."

作者的話

賽皮喜歡跳上跳下，他會跳到椅子上，然後從椅子上跳到桌上，最後再從桌上跳到沙發上。有時候，他甚至會跳到冰箱上面去呢！

我很喜歡馬戲團。當我看到賽皮跳來跳去的時候，我覺得他看起來就像隻「馬戲團的貓」。

❀ About the Author

Carla Golembe is the illustrator of thirteen children's books, five of which she wrote. Carla has won several awards including a New York Times Best Illustrated Picture Book Award. She has also received illustration awards from Parents' Choice and the American Folklore Society. She has twenty-five years of college teaching experience and, for the last thirteen years, has given speaker presentations and workshops to elementary schools. She lives in Southeast Florida, with her husband Joe and her cats Zippy and Zoe.

❀ 關於作者

Carla Golembe 擔任過十三本童書的繪者，其中五本是由她寫作的。Carla 曾多次獲獎，包括《紐約時報》最佳圖畫書獎。她也曾獲全美父母首選基金會，以及美國民俗學會的插畫獎項。她有二十五年的大學教學經驗，而在過去的十三年中，曾經在多所小學中演講及舉辦研討會。她目前和丈夫 Joe 以及她的貓——賽皮與柔依，住在美國佛羅里達州東南部。

寶皮與柔依系列

ZIPPY AND ZOE SERIES

想知道寶皮和柔依發生了什麼驚奇又爆笑的事嗎？
歡迎學習英文本0-2年的小朋友一起來分享我們的故事——
「寶皮與柔依系列」，讓你在一連串有趣的事情中學英文！

精裝／附中英雙語朗讀CD／全套六本

Carla Golembe 著／繪

本局編輯部 譯

Hello！ 我是寶皮，我喜歡畫畫、做餅乾，還有跟柔依一起去海邊玩。偷偷告訴你，我在馬戲團表演過呢！

Hi， 我是柔依，今年最開心的事，就是寶皮送我一張他親手畫的生日卡片！寶皮是我最要好的朋友，他很聰明也很可愛，我們兩個常常一起出去玩。

寶皮與柔依系列有

1 寶皮與綠色顏料
(Zippy and the Green Paint)

2 寶皮與馬戲團
(Zippy and the Circus)

3 寶皮與超級大餅乾
(Zippy and the Very Big Cookie)

4 寶皮做運動
(Zippy Chooses a Sport)

5 寶皮學認字
(Zippy Reads)

6 寶皮與柔依去海邊
(Zippy and Zoe Go to the Beach)

國家圖書館出版品預行編目資料

Zippy and the Circus:賽皮與馬戲團 / Carla
Golembe著;Carla Golembe繪;本局編輯部譯.－
－初版一刷.－－臺北市：三民，2006
　　面；　　公分.－－(Fun心讀雙語叢書.賽皮與柔
　　依系列)
中英對照
ISBN 957－14－4451－0　　(精裝)

1.英國語言－讀本

523.38　　　　　　　　　　　　　　94026565

網路書店位址　http://www.sanmin.com.tw

© **Zippy and the Circus**
──賽皮與馬戲團

著作人	Carla Golembe
繪　者	Carla Golembe
譯　者	本局編輯部
發行人	劉振強
著作財產權人	三民書局股份有限公司 臺北市復興北路386號
發行所	三民書局股份有限公司 地址／臺北市復興北路386號 電話／(02)25006600 郵撥／0009998－5
印刷所	三民書局股份有限公司
門市部	復北店／臺北市復興北路386號 重南店／臺北市重慶南路一段61號
初版一刷	2006年1月
編　號	S 806181
定　價	新臺幣壹佰捌拾元整

行政院新聞局登記證局版臺業字第〇二〇〇號

ISBN　957－14－4451－0　　(精裝)